A Guide
For Grievers

Bob Willis

Bob Willis

Blessings.
III John 2

ISBN# 978-1545560686

Subject Headings:
Grief, Self-Help, Counseling

DEDICATION

A Guide For Grievers is dedicated to those who have touched my life with their broken hearts...shared their stories and their tears...mourned openly...and taught me the value of having a guide through this very difficult journey called grief.

CONTENTS

UNDERSTANDING GRIEF

Get a good education...get some more education...get a good job...get a perfect mate...get a nice house...get a new car...get a better job...get more ...get...get...get!

We are taught to accumulate things in life. We are not taught to lose things, especially people. No one taught us to cope with loss.

The purpose of this book is to provide a guide to someone who has experienced the loss of a loved one. During this time of heartache, it is often difficult to find helpful direction and comforting guidance. This book will provide insight into the normal responses to a loss, reveal the impact of loss upon a myriad of areas in life, and provide a way to help bring comfort from the seemingly endless waves of pain.

Grievers who have recently lost a loved one through death have been living in a fog. In the midst of this thick and relentless fog, there were funeral arrangements to be made, family members and friends to be contacted, searching for documents and paperwork, answering endless questions, trying to get rest in small windows of time, greeting visitors, and countless other tasks forced upon the bereaved.

Finally, the necessary tasks are completed, the funeral is over, and everyone seems to be going back to a routine. The telephone calls have slowed down, family members have returned to their lives, and visits from friends are becoming less frequent. But, you realize your life will never be the same again. So this book is meant to identify the feelings of the moment, and provide some guidance to answer the question..."Now what?"

One of the primary tasks for those experiencing a loss is to acknowledge that the loss has actually occurred. It is impossible to move along on a grief journey until this task has been accomplished. Not only is it important for the griever to acknowledge the loss, but it is also very important for others to acknowledge the loss with them. This is usually accomplished at a funeral or memorial service for the loved one. The griever knows their loved one was significant to them, what helps them is when they hear how significant their loved one was to others. It lends value to the life that was lived, provides confirmation that the life was not lived in vain.

Grief is a complex accumulation of intense emotions. Grief is often described as emptiness, loneliness, pain, heartache, a void, even a deep longing.

Mourning is the outward expression of the grief felt within. These expressions might be in the form of tears, angry outbursts, or words.

It is impossible to see another person's grief. Grief is personal and private for each person. No one grieves in the same manner, even if they are part of the same family experiencing the same changes. We grieve according to our personality, the closeness of our relationships, and other losses in our life. The way we react to changes and respond to losses in life are as unique as our fingerprint. When feelings of grief are expressed openly, they become mourning. A good definition of mourning is "grief gone public". When we see someone cry following a loss, we do not see their grief, but we are observing the outward expression of the inward pain, we are seeing them mourn. It is very healthy to express the feelings and pain of grief, for then it becomes mourning.

2
A Guide to Normal Responses

This is not intended to be a checklist of normal responses following a loss. Nor is it meant to be a complete list of responses. But, if you have experienced the death of a loved one, do not be surprised if you can identify with many of these responses. Identifying with these responses is meant to lower the anxiety level by confirming you are on the same journey of grief traveled by millions of others. You are normal!

- <u>Numb to people and events around you, feeling out of place</u>

It is very normal to be in shock after a loss. Your thought process has changed. You may hear words but not understand their meaning. It is as if you are a stranger, not even connected to the events around you.

- A feeling of tightness in the throat or heaviness in the chest

Grief impacts us physically as well as emotionally, mentally, and spiritually. Our entire system has taken a very hard hit and the shock of it can impact breathing, sleeping, even our energy level. Having a complete medical physical can provide peace of mind at this time.

- A feeling of emptiness in the stomach and change in eating habits

Grief is gut-wrenching. There may be stomach pains resembling hunger pains. Some people cannot eat anything at this time,...food might not sound good, taste good, or even smell good. Others can eat everything in sight, almost a nervous feeding frenzy. There needs to be a balance between these two extremes because the body does need nutrition to maintain the level of strength required to function each day.

- Feelings of restlessness and difficulty concentrating

We lose people physically, we never lose them emotionally or spiritually. So, to be as close as we can be to our loved one who died, we do not need to visit the gravesite. We get close to them when we visit memories. Our mind and thoughts will be upon the memories, even if they are painful to us. When our mind is focused on the past, we lose the ability to concentrate on the present. It may be very difficult to sit still or remain in one location for an extended period of time. Remember, our mind is in shock and it takes extra effort to focus and concentrate upon daily tasks and routines.

- <u>Feeling as though the loss isn't real, that it is a bad dream</u>

What you are hearing, seeing, and experiencing can feel like a bad dream...even a nightmare. It is normal to think you will just wake up and everything will be different. This is a typical part of denial and will resolve as the facts and reality become even more evident.

- <u>Wandering aimlessly and forgetting to finish projects</u>

Do not be surprised if you have several projects started, with nothing completed. This relates to the inability to concentrate or focus. Making a list of simple tasks and remaining with one until you can cross it off the list may help overcome this uneasy feeling.

- <u>Sleeping patterns change</u>

Because our system has been hit with such shock, the ability to relax and sleep might be absent. Sleeping patterns for caregivers had already changed. There will be a new normal for sleeping but it might take months to develop. Sleeping the majority of the time, not getting dressed or attending to personal care might be a sign of depression. It might be helpful to see a physician for guidance in the area of sleeplessness.

- Dreaming of our loved one, or NOT dreaming of them are both normal

Remember, we do not lose the emotional or spiritual aspects of our relationship. When asleep, we surrender control of our thoughts. Dreaming of a loved one who died can often be comforting, but not dreaming of them can also be normal. Before going to sleep, voice a prayer for God to provide a comforting dream of your loved one if He thinks you require that assurance and comfort.

- Experience a preoccupation with memories of the deceased

Memories are left behind when a loved one dies. It is quite normal for grievers to surround themselves with material items (photos, clothing, handiwork, etc.) that connect them to their loved one. Suddenly these reminders become treasures because of the connection to a loved one who is no longer physically present.

- Assume mannerisms, traits, or roles of the loved one

The absence of a loved one due to death can leave a void in the family system. Someone might step forward to fulfill the role left vacant, or continue a trait or mannerism of the deceased. This can be an effort for their memory to continue, recognizing the importance of their role.

- <u>Feelings of guilt or regret over things that did or didn't happen in the relationship with the deceased</u>

Guilt and regret are both normal responses following a death. But, there is a difference. Guilt can develop following a decision we made knowing what the outcome would be. Regret can be felt due to the actions or words that just happened in the relationship. If we could go back, we would have done things differently. Both of these feelings are normal and it is possible to learn healthy ways to express each one.

- <u>Feelings of intense anger at the loved one, at God, doctors, etc</u>

Anger is normal during a time of loss, it is a normal response to the helplessness being experienced. We may be angry at the person who died if we feel they could have changed the outcome. Doctors, hospitals, even other family members can become the target of our anger. Anger at a time of loss serves to vent the loss of control in the entire situation.

- <u>Feeling abandoned by the loved one</u>

Death can rob a couple of the ability to live out their dreams. A promise to grow old together can feel broken and meaningless at this time. The loss of a mate or another supportive relationship can feel like abandonment because the relationship had not been completed.

- <u>Feeling a need to protect others by not talking about the loss</u>

It is normal to try and protect children and others in the family by not discussing the loss. In reality, an open communication of feelings is much healthier. It is impossible for one person to protect the feelings and emotions of another person.

- <u>Needing to tell, retell, and remember stories of the loved one and the experience of their death</u>

The ability to share memories and stories is a very healthy aspect in the grief process. This can be a healing time of laughter and tears, a time of honoring the life of a loved one. Grievers need to talk, they just need a safe place and a safe person available to them. Sharing the circumstances surrounding the death can help to confirm the reality of the event.

- <u>Mood changes over the slightest things, having some good moments and some bad moments</u>

Give yourself permission to laugh and cry. Grief is like riding an emotional roller coaster, with highs and lows. You cannot predict when the next memory might appear unexpectedly, and it can change your mood instantly. We do not live one day at a time, but actually one moment at a time.

- <u>Tears at unexpected times</u>

We expect to cry at a funeral, or while visiting the cemetery, or while sharing memories of our loved one. We do not expect to cry in the grocery store, or while driving a car, but it will happen. Give yourself permission to experience tears. These are very healthy times of venting the emotions of grief.

 # A Rest Stop

Wash Day Grief

Have you ever looked at the settings on your washing machine as they relate to grief? Consider these common washing machine settings:

NORMAL: Normal responses following a loss may include mood changes, changes in eating and sleeping patterns, feelings of anger, abandonment, despair, loss of concentration, loss of energy, and the loss of motivation. These responses can vary based upon previous loss experiences, our relationships, and even our personality.

SMALL LOAD: Each person's grief is a major life event. However, there may be some days the grief pain is not as intense. These days offer the time to catch your breath. Regardless of the relationship...regardless of the circumstances surrounding the loss...it is a major loss.

LARGE LOAD: Grief can bring on very intense feelings. These feelings can be overwhelming, even to someone with a history of always being under control.

We can be paralyzed emotionally because of the shock a loss brings.

SPIN CYCLE: Several events can throw a griever into a "spin cycle". Holidays, birthdays, anniversaries, photos, music, food, and even fragrances can begin the "spin cycle" of emotions. These are normal twists and turns along the journey of grief.

RINSE CYCLE: The rinse cycle is a time of refreshing. Tears provide a natural rinsing, a cleansing of the soul. Grief encompasses all of the confusing and painful emotions felt after a loss. Mourning is the outward expression of these feelings...whether through tears, words, or actions.

COOL DOWN: No one can take grief away. Expressing grief to a safe person, or becoming part of a grief support group, can provide a "cool down" time. These steps can help soften the pain of grief, but the awareness of the loss will remain.

Give yourself permission to be a "NORMAL" griever. Some days will bring a "SMALL LOAD" of grief...other days will consist of a "LARGE LOAD". The "SPIN CYCLE" may be intense at times...while the "RINSE CYCLE" of tears can cleanse the soul as we mourn the loss. Peace and acceptance can offer a "COOL DOWN" phase...a time of rest.

3
A Guide to Secondary Losses

Have you ever thrown a stone into a pool of still water? If so, you can recall how the stone disappeared. But from the point it contacted the surface of the water there were circular ripples extending outward from the center. These ripples would have never appeared if the stone had not interrupted the calmness of the water. This is a picture of the grief process and the subsequent reminders of a loss. When the loss occurred, the "stone" entered into the calm of your life. The impact of a stone into the water seems to create a hole in the water that is quickly covered up by the ripples. The impact of your loss can make it feel like a hole in your heart, only to have ripples of pain overwhelm your peace. These ripples are secondary losses. They may be produced by the awareness of birthdates, holidays, anniversaries, seeing a photograph of a loved one, or even hearing a favorite song. These, and many other reminders, make us aware of many "secondary losses" connected to our primary loss. We may also experience the...

• Loss of JOY

When faced with the reality of a loved one's death, we seem to lose the joy and laughter once experienced with them. Joy can disappear and leave behind a painful silence. We wonder if we will ever experience joy and laughter again in our life. Our reason for joy has died.

• Loss of BALANCE

The support and encouragement we receive from others can provide the balance to assure our stability in life. Emotional balance can be the hug without words, the nod of support and encouragement, someone to serve as our emotional compass.

• Loss of DREAMS

Relationships end before we are through with them. "We always planned to..." is verbalized as a realization that dreams die too. There can be a feeling of being cheated or robbed when a relationship ends. Dreaming again can be difficult, and it may take time to develop.

• Loss of CONTROL

If you could control things, your loved one would be healthy and enjoying life. Now it is difficult to control sleeping, eating, or even thinking. Give yourself permission to lose control of your emotions at this time. Find a safe place and a safe person who will allow you to express these feelings. You will start gaining control again, moment by moment.

- Loss of INTIMACY

The loss of the physical aspect in a relationship, the intimacy that formed a bond of trust, is often overlooked in the grief process. This emptiness, this void, is intensified with the realization that the person you had given yourself to totally is no longer present with you.

- Loss of SUPPORT

A support system is having that person you can rely upon to be there for you, someone to draw strength from, providing a sense of safety. When that person is gone, there can be a sense of being vulnerable and helpless.

- Loss of SECURITY

We find security at many levels. Physical security might involve having someone's presence and protection; financial security can be the assurance of assets and being financially comfortable in life; emotional security can be having a safe person we can share everything with. The loss, or change, in any of these areas can intensify the grief responses.

- Loss of SELF ESTEEM

Often we draw our self esteem from others who instill worth and value into our life. If that person is gone, our worth and value will be impacted. The challenge is to believe in our abilities, even if no one is there to affirm us.

- Loss of MOTIVATION

Grief can paralyze us emotionally. Our desire to return to a normal or routine schedule will be absent. It's common to pull into a shell, avoiding people and responsibilities. There can be a complete lack of interest in anything, even those things we enjoyed before the loss.

- Loss of ENERGY

Grief is exhausting work. It's hard work...and it is heart work. Your physical and emotional energy levels can be drained. You can feel empty. It is difficult to provide support to others when you are emotionally drained.

- Loss of PURPOSE

Perhaps you were an excellent caregiver for your loved one. You did a great job of providing for them physically and emotionally. Now that death has occurred...what do you do now? It's like being great at your job, and then suddenly you are unemployed. Where do you go from here?

- Loss of UNCONDITIONAL LOVE

You may have lost the only person who has ever loved you unconditionally. Unconditional love says, "I love you... regardless... period". It is not critical or judgmental.

- ## Loss of the FUTURE

When a loss occurs, it is very difficult to look into the future. It's difficult to make long term plans while surviving moment to moment. Future plans involved the presence of a loved one who is no longer available. There will be times to re-dream, to make long term plans. These plans will be different because your life is different now.

- ## Loss of a SAFE PERSON

There are times we need a safe person in our life. They are the unique person who will lend us their ears, and not their mouth. We confide in them, share hurts and secrets with them, knowing it is safe for eternity. When that person dies, we have a deep sense of being abandoned, and our safe outlet is not available. It takes time to find and develop a safe person relationship, but it's worth the effort.

- ## Loss of a BEST FRIEND

We need someone who is comfortable with our laughter and our tears. Our best friend gets to see and know the "real" person. When they die, or the relationship changes, our walls of safety might go up to provide security for our heart.

- ## Loss of a CHEERLEADER

When we face challenges or struggles in life, we need someone who really believes in us, someone who encourages us. We need a cheerleader. Someone in that role can provide the support and strength for us to achieve our greatest potential. When that person dies, we may question our ability to meet challenges. We miss the person who encouraged us when we had doubts . Be open to another cheerleader, someone who steps in to believe in you.

- Loss of <u>EXPECTATIONS</u>

We grieve the loss of what should have been, what might have been, or what could have been. We lose our expectations of how things should have developed in life. This can shake everything about our belief system. It will be difficult for us to expect outcomes anymore in life.

- Loss of <u>NORMAL</u>

What was once normal will never be normal again. There will be a new normal...but it will be different. Living your life without the presence of your loved one will never feel normal. Now it is normal to feel the emptiness, the loneliness, and the awareness that part of your heart is missing.

A Rest Stop

Speed Bumps

Have you ever driven across a parking lot and hit a little speed bump placed there to control the speed of traffic? No matter the speed we are traveling, it hurts. It shakes everything within us. We decide immediately to slow down and watch for speed bumps because it hurt too much and we do not want that to happen again.

Every relationship has its share of speed bumps. Things can happen in relationships that shakes everything within us. These speed bumps may be a lack of communication, broken promises, loss of trust, neglect, poor choices, oversight, etc. When these events occur we usually decide to slow down and pay closer attention to the relationship. Hitting the speed bump hurt too much, and we don't want it to happen again. The pain of the event may cause us to be more sensitive to others and anticipate the impact of our choices. We begin to recognize the speed bumps and make deliberate adjustments to avoid the pain.

It is easy to live life without consideration of others and the impact our decisions might have on them. We are often so focused on making a living that we overlook the important things in life. It is true: the important things in life are not things at all

... they are relationships. When faced with a crisis in life, a chronic or terminal illness, the loss of a valuable relationship, the failure of a dream, or a hundred other life events ... the entire picture can change. Priorities in life change. What was once very important to us in life can move to the bottom of the priority list. Also, those things that seemed to always be the least important to us have a way of suddenly moving to the top of the list. Our perspective on life, the way we view it, changes. This might be a great time for us to slow down and watch for speed bumps in the relationships we treasure.

4
A Guide to Honor A Relationship

They were only in their 50's when Ben Ann's husband died. They were not through with this relationship; they had many plans for the years ahead. In a grief support group, Ben Ann made this statement…"I know my husband was not perfect, but he was perfect for me. He completed my life, and since his death I have been incomplete!". This powerful statement is so true. There are no perfect people, but there are people who complete our life. They fill the emptiness, they provide the balance, they share the dreams, they pick us up when we fall…they fulfill our life. When that person is no longer with us it leaves a very painful and empty place in our life. The following exercise provides a way to honor the life of that special person. Write your responses to these three areas. There are no wrong answers; these are your memories, your way to honor this special relationship.

- What is the earliest memory you have of them?

- What is a memory that feels good when you recall them?

- What is a memory that hurts when you recall them?

 A Rest Stop

Listening With "P-R-A-Y-E-R

Presence: Be present with the griever. Listen to their every word...do not use their "speaking time" as your "prep time" on what to say next. Allow them to vent their feelings...all of them. Maintain eye contact with them as much as possible.

Restate: Summarize their statements and repeat them back to confirm you are hearing their true feelings. They will correct you if the meaning has not been clearly understood. By clarifying their feeling statements, you are supporting them in their grief.

Ask: Use open ended questions to deepen the conversation and allow them to express even more feelings. Your follow-up questions will indicate they are being heard...and that you are really listening to their heart.

Yield: This time is not about you...it's about the griever and their feelings. Do not attempt to minimize the pain of their grief by comparing it to other losses. Do not appear to be in a hurry, rushed, or distracted by time. Make them your priority.

Empathize: Join them in their grief pain. Use open body language, not closed off. Nod your head as they share...this indicates you are with them on their painful journey. It is okay to shed tears with them... an indication you have heard their feelings.

Resist: Resist the urge to change the subject or cut the conversation off prematurely. Instead of telling them how they should feel, allow grievers to share their real feelings at this time.

5

A Guide to Express Feelings

Often death robs us of the opportunity to say things to our loved one. We always think we have tomorrow, or next week, or next year, to express our feelings to them. But, death can step in and the relationship ends before we are through with it. When our loved one dies, we usually stuff these feelings into the maze and uncertainty of our grief pain.

This exercise allows these feelings to be identified, organized, and expressed. Imagine you had the opportunity to talk with your loved one again. The following statements may provide the avenue to express the feelings of grief that have been suppressed, stuffed, or denied for years. For each of them, write as much as you desire in order to express the true feelings of your heart. These statements are not what others think you should say, but a true expression of your heart. Of course, if a statement does not elicit a response, please move on to the next statement. This list serves as a guide for expressing the emotions of grief. The responses will be different for each person.

Find a private and quiet place where you can write without being disturbed. Some of this process might be emotional, so prepare for the healthy expression of emotions. Read the statements and write as much as you can in a personal journal, expressing your true feelings. You will know when you are through, when you have nothing else to write.

Dear _____,

"I want to thank you for...." You may have expressed appreciation and gratitude to your loved one before they died, but there may be a need to say some things again. Write these down as if you were talking to them one more time.

"My fondest memory of you is..." This could be a memory that brings a smile, laughter, or even tears. But, it is a treasure because it involves your loved one. Describe this memory as completely and accurately as possible.

"I feel good when I think of..." This is an opportunity to express those things that happened in the relationship that are comforting to think of. Memories that feel good are the high points in a relationship.

"I hurt when I think of..." This could put words to the deep pain within your heart. As you review your relationship, there may be things you remember that bring pain to you, things you wish had not happened. Express them here.

"I want to apologize to you for..." There may be something weighing heavy upon your heart, something you would apologize to your loved one if you could talk with them again. Even if you had expressed this before, if it is still heavy on your heart it needs to be expressed again.

"I forgive you for..." Forgiveness is giving up the hope of a different or better yesterday. It is not saying what is right or wrong, or who is to blame. Expressing forgiveness is realizing you cannot continue to carry the burden of holding a grudge or an attitude of un-forgiveness. This is an opportunity to express these feelings, time to put past hurts where they belong...in the past.

"I wish I had..." These are regrets in a relationship. This is the place to express things we would have said or done differently if we could go back in the relationship. Often we are so busy living life or being in the caregiver role, that we do not take time to say or do the most important things. This is the place to write these feelings.

"I feel guilty when I think of..." Guilt can come following an intentional decision when we know what the outcome will be. If you feel guilty because of something that was said or done, this is the place to write it down. Guilt can become a very heavy load and it needs to be identified and expressed in order to find comfort in the grief process.

"I get angry when..." Anger is a normal part of grief. We can be angry at our loved one for their actions or their neglect. We can be angry at ourselves, at doctors, and even angry at God. This is the place to put your anger into words.

"I always wanted to tell you..." Relationships often end unexpectedly and leave us with unfinished business. Sickness and death can rob us of the opportunity or the time to say important things to our loved one. What would you say to them now?

"I would like to have heard you say..." Grief is not always what we say or do. Often we grieve what we did not hear from our loved one before they died. If you could talk with them again, what would you like for them to say to you? What do you need to hear from them?

"I want you to know..." This is the opportunity to express any of the grief feelings that did not seem to fit into any of the previous statements. It is a way to express the pain being suppressed. This area can contain statements on any aspect of the relationship, or any unfinished business.

Once you have written everything you would like to include in this letter, there is another very important step to take.

Look for a safe person in your life, someone who will allow you to read these statements without being judgmental or critical. This may be someone outside of family, but it will be someone who will listen to you, even if it gets emotional during the process.

This guide provides a way to identify the grief, organize it under headings, and mourn or express the grief. This can be a very emotional exercise, but please realize it is okay to express these emotions. This provides a healthy way to let it out...to mourn the grief.

A Rest Stop

The Wrapper

A fatal heart attack had suddenly removed a man from the family circle who served as husband, father, father-in-law, grandfather, and a multitude of other special relationships. A few days following the funeral service, I met with the family members for a special time of remembrance.

We talked about the good memories of the deceased, the happy times shared by the family over the years. These stories brought forth tears of laughter and tears of sorrow. But, nonetheless, it was a time of healing for all involved. In our family meeting, we discovered the healing qualities of sharing precious memories.

A beautiful illustration was given by a daughter-in law during the family session. I have shared this story many times since, always with a tremendous amount of appreciation for the truth it sets forth. Here is the account as it was shared with me.

Following the death and the funeral service, her four-year-old son came to her and asked, "Where is Grandpa?" She gently told him "Grandpa died." The young boy looked at her even more intently and asked, "Where is Grandpa now?" The young mother gently responded "Grandpa is in heaven." A look of satisfaction crossed the young boy's face, and he quietly went to bed for the night.

The next morning, the family members drove to the cemetery to see the grave. Everyone got out of the car, walked to the edge of the grave which was completely covered with flowers. The four-year-old boy approached the mound of flowers, turned to his mother and asked, "Is this heaven?"

The mother felt helpless for an answer to the young boy's honest question. How could she explain to him the difference between Grandpa being in heaven, and visiting Grandpa's grave?

That evening she sat on the edge of her young son's bed and took a candy bar from her pocket. The boy's eyes lit up as she opened the wrapper to reveal the chocolate treat inside. She broke off a chunk of the candy bar, handed it to the boy and said, "Let's talk about Grandpa. What good memories do you have of Grandpa?" The excitement was obvious as he told how Grandpa had taken him fishing, they had gone to the zoo together, they had even gone to a baseball game together! The whole time he shared these happy memories, he was enjoying more and more of the candy bar.

As the good memories and the candy bar were finished, the young mother snuggled up close to the boy, gave him a big hug, and said, "You know son,

Grandpa is a lot like this candy bar. The good, delicious, wonderful, and enjoyable part of Grandpa that you remember, that's the part of Grandpa that's in heaven."

Then, holding up the empty candy bar wrapper, she said, "This is the part of Grandpa that's buried in the ground ... just Grandpa's wrapper." A look of delight swept over the young boy's face as he realized the enjoyable part of people is never forgotten. What seemed like a puzzle hours before became a clear picture of the new relationship possible with those who die.

6

A Guide to Friends

In our death defying society we use various terms to speak of a death without actually saying the word. We talk of someone "passing on", "expired", "Gone to heaven", etc. instead of saying the obvious... they died. We speak the truth when we talk of a plant that has died, or a pet that died, but for some reason it's more difficult to use that word when a person dies.

Having open and frank conversations about the feelings that can be identified will be a tremendous help. When we mention we lost our job, lost our home, or lost our car, people usually ask "what happened?" A very appropriate and healing comment when someone shares they have lost a loved one would simply be to ask..."what happened?". We can then allow them to express their feelings and relate their story to us.

Actions and comments can be very helpful. Many times it is not what we say to someone in grief as much as it is just being present with them.

A woman was diagnosed with cancer and was visited by a friend who made the following statement: "I don't know what to say to you, I don't know what to do for you. What do YOU need from me?" This gave the woman control of the conversation and she was able to express what she needed. Hugs are good, grievers need more of them, but someone who will simply provide a listening ear will be of great value. People in grief are not broken, so they do not need anyone attempting to "fix" them with words.

What grievers would like their friends to know...

It HELPS when someone...

- <u>INCLUDES ME</u>

It hurts when a loved one dies. The pain of loss is magnified when it seems everyone just walks away at that time also. Contact me; try to include me in some activities. I might decline, but at least I know you haven't forgotten about me.

- ## MENTIONS THE NAME OF MY LOVED ONE

The mention of their name might bring tears or laughter. It's okay either way. Their name did not die; I live with it every moment of every day.

- ## SHARES A MEMORY OF MY LOVED ONE

I know they were significant to me... it helps immensely to hear how significant they were to others. Let me share my stories and my memories also, without having you walk away or change the subject.

- ## SENDS A CARD OR CALLS ON THEIR BIRTHDAY

Birthdays are still on the calendar and it is a reminder of their absence. If you send a card, enclose a memory of them. That will be a gift to me on that special day.

- ## SENDS A CARD OR CALLS ON A HOLIDAY

Holidays and the traditions surrounding them can be extremely difficult. I may need to be absent from a lot of the holiday activity. Just a card to acknowledge you are thinking of me, and my loved one, at this time can be comforting.

- ## OFFERS TO DO PRACTICAL ERRANDS FOR ME

Some of the simple tasks seem so difficult, even impossible, for the griever. The role my loved one filled had tasks that are new and strange territory for me. Offer to guide or instruct me.

- ## OFFERS TO ATTEND A GRIEF GROUP WITH ME

Grief groups are not a sign of weakness, but a place to gain valuable support. Attending a grief group alone is a big step. It will add courage if someone offers to go with me for support.

- ## OFFERS TO TAKE FLOWERS TO THE CEMETERY WITH ME

Sometimes I need a safe friend who will go with me to the cemetery. Someone who will allow me to cry and share memories, even express all types of emotions.

It HURTS when someone says...

- ## I KNOW JUST HOW YOU FEEL

It is impossible for anyone to know just how I feel. No one had the same relationship with my loved one. Everyone grieves differently, according to our personality, other losses in our life, even the level of our relationship with the person who died.

- ## YOU SHOULD BE OVER THIS BY NOW

I'll never "get over it". Grief is not like a cold you just get over. We lose people physically, but emotionally and spiritually we never lose them.

- <u>THEY WOULD NOT WANT YOU TO CRY</u>

Grief is the pain on the inside, crying is a way of expressing the pain. When I express my grief pain it becomes mourning. I believe my loved one would want me to be comforted by mourning their loss...it's healthy...it's Scriptural.

- <u>IT WAS GOD'S WILL</u>

I resent that statement! I realize God is never surprised by anything that happens, and I am aware He will never leave me. Determining God's will is a personal thing and this response seems to be a weak attempt to justify the end of someone's life.

- <u>HE/SHE IS HAPPY NOW</u>

This implies they were not happy with me in our relationship. It makes it sound as if their death allowed them to escape from me and an unhappy relationship.

- <u>YOU MUST BE STRONG FOR THE CHILDREN</u>

Children need to see adults grieving and mourning in healthy ways. Hiding feelings from children confuses them on what to do with their own feelings. Seeing an adult cry gives children permission to express and talk about their feelings also.

- <u>YOU HAVE TO GET AHOLD OF YOURSELF</u>

Grief is a confusing mass of intense emotions. Normal has changed drastically, in every aspect of life. There will be a new normal but it may take awhile to find it, and when it arrives it may not be received gracefully.

- <u>YOU ARE DOING SO WELL</u>

You can't see my grief...it's on the inside. My moods will change quickly; I will go from laughter to tears. Its okay if you think I'm "doing well"...as long as you give me permission to "not do well" at times also.

- <u>YOU ARE NOT YOURSELF ANYMORE</u>

Thank you for noticing. A big part of my heart has been ripped out, so I am not the same. Everything in my life has changed, it does not mean that it is wrong, it is just different. I'm learning to live moment by moment with a big empty place in my heart.

- <u>IT JUST TAKES TIME</u>

How long? 6 months? A year? Two or three years? I believe grief takes a lifetime. Grief does not go by a set schedule of events, or a calendar. To me there are 3 stages of grief: intense pain, painful, and not as painful.

A Rest Stop

Identifying Supportive People

A supportive person will be someone who accepts you without being judgmental. They let you describe your feelings, and they understand your circumstances and how they impact each area of your life. They are at your side, supporting you to do whatever is important and best for you. They will allow you to ask why without feeling they must provide an answer. List the people who make up your support system. Identify the safe people who will be available to you physically, emotionally, and spiritually. Write their name and telephone numbers below...

7

A Guide to Special Days

Birthdays, anniversaries, and holidays can be very painful following the death of a loved one. Family traditions are changed forever, and it can be very difficult to face a special event in the midst of grief. There are actually two options for a griever. We can make no plans and feel depressed and defeated when the special day arrives. Or, we can take the initiative and make plans to honor our loved one on this special day.

Here are some suggestions to honor loved ones on special days and holidays. Use this as a springboard to develop your own unique way to honor their memory.

New Years Day

• Make a list of "first experiences" you shared with your loved one

• Plan ways to honor your loved one throughout the year

• Begin a "bucket list"...things you would like to accomplish in the upcoming year

• Be open to meeting a "new friend" this upcoming year...someone who will allow you to laugh and cry around them

• Donate money in memory of your loved one to an organization that helps restore addicts to a new life...offering them a new beginning

Valentine's Day

• Write a love letter to your loved one to express gratitude and listing all the things you loved about them. Consider reading the letter aloud at their graveside, or to a safe person

• Send a Valentine's Day card to your family members, expressing at least one thing you love about each one of them

• Place fresh flowers at your loved one's grave

• Donate money in memory of your loved one to the American Heart Association, or to another favorite charity

Easter

• Visit your loved one's grave at sunrise on Easter morning and read the account of the resurrection of Christ from the Bible (John 19:31-20:18)

• Attend a worship service to hear the message of hope in the resurrection

- Plan an Easter lunch with family or friends

- Donate Easter lilies to a church in memory of your loved one

Mother's Day

- Attend a church service to honor all mothers

- Make a list of "treasures from mother"...things she passed down to family

- Display photos of your loved one along with some of their personal possessions

- Donate money in memory of your mother to an abused woman's shelter or a home for unwed mothers

Father's Day

- Involve family members in an activity your loved one would have enjoyed

- Display photos and keepsakes connected to their memory

- Spend time researching family history and gathering photographs

- Donate money in memory of your father to an organization that helps boys who do not have a father figure in their life

Memorial Day

- Visit the cemetery to place fresh flowers, flags, and decorations

- Revisit favorite places you enjoyed with your loved one

- Plant a tree in memory of your loved one

- Donate money in memory of your loved one to the Alzheimer's Association or another favorite charity working with those who have memory loss

Independence Day

- Proudly display the American flag at your home

- Talk with a friend about the freedoms enjoyed in this country

- Attend a parade, picnic, or fireworks display with family or friends

- Donate money in memory of your loved one to an organization furnishing Bibles to men and women who are incarcerated

Veteran's Day

- Mail a letter of encouragement to a serviceman or woman from your hometown

- Visit a veterans hospital to encourage families and patients

- Display photos of your loved one in service

- Donate money in memory of your loved one to a program in your community that is assisting veterans

Labor Day

- Compliment someone for doing a "good job"
- Give clothing to an organization helping the underprivileged
- Take cookies to a local fire department or police station in appreciation of their work to serve the public
- Donate money in memory of your loved one to a local organization of community volunteers

Thanksgiving Day

- Serve meals to the homeless at a community organization
- Adopt a needy person or family and provide a Thanksgiving meal to them
- Donate money in memory of your loved one to an organization that feeds the homeless people throughout the year
- At your Thanksgiving celebration...provide a white table cloth and permanent markers. Ask everyone to write something on the tablecloth they are thankful for, including a signature and date. Carefully store the tablecloth and repeat the tradition each year

Christmas Day

- Write or share favorite Christmas memories that involved your loved one

- Adopt a needy person or family and provide Christmas gifts for them

- Invite someone to your Christmas meal who cannot be with their family this year

- Donate money in memory of your loved one to a local organization that furnishes toys for needy children

Birthdays and Wedding Anniversaries

- Have a birthday party for your loved one. Invite a few family and friends, share memories and photos together, enjoy their favorite food.

- Attach love notes to helium filled balloons and release them

- Plant a tree in a prominent location in memory of your loved one

- Place stepping stones in a flower garden with their name inscribed on the stone

- Donate money in their memory to an organization that provides counseling and marriage enrichment to couples

 # A Rest Stop

Are You Facing Toward Me?

It was a devastating death in the rural community. The young wife died suddenly, leaving behind her husband and a son. There was a great outpouring of sympathy for the family. The small church had an overflow crowd at her funeral.

Following the service, family and friends gathered in the home to offer comfort to the husband and son. It was late when everyone left the home. The father and young son found themselves alone in the home for the first time. As bedtime approached, the dad tucked his son into bed, hugged him tightly, and said "I love you son. I love you." As he left the room, he turned the light off, and it grew very dark in that part of the house.

After the dad settled into his own bed, he reached over and turned the lamp off. It was quiet and dark in the house. In just a few minutes he heard the voice of his son, "Daddy, can I come sleep with you?" Realizing the difficult time they were both having, he went to his son's room and carried him to his own room.

After they settled into the bed, dad reached over and turned off the lamp again. It was so dark in the house, it was impossible to see even the form of the young boy in his arms. In a few minutes the quietness was broken again with the voice of the boy, "Daddy, are you facing toward me?" Dad said, "Yes, son, I'm facing toward you. Why are you asking?" "Because it's real dark, and I'm afraid," said the young boy. "If I know you are facing toward me I think I can rest and go to sleep." In just a few short minutes, the dad could tell his son had fallen asleep in his arms.

Moved by the simple trust of his son, the father laid his head back upon his pillow and looked up to Heaven. "Father, are you facing toward me?" he asked. "It's real dark in my world right now, and I'm afraid. If I know you are facing toward me, I think I can rest and go to sleep."

This story illustrates the truth of God's presence. Even when you can't see Him or feel Him, He is there. As a caregiver or a care-receiver, there will be times of darkness and fear, but He is always facing toward you.

Contact Bob Willis for...

- Speaking opportunities
- Comments/questions about A Guide For Grievers
- A free support group leaders guide using A Guide For Grievers book

Email: Bob@Godhealshearts.com

Website: www.Godhealshearts.com

Phone: (405) 808-6925

Made in the USA
Monee, IL
08 September 2022

12530175R00036